Seven-Star Bird

Seven-Star
BIRD

POEMS BY

David Daniel

Graywolf Press
SAINT PAUL, MINNESOTA

Publication of this volume is made possible in part by a grant provided by the Minnesota State Arts Board, through an appropriation by the Minnesota State Legislature; a grant from the Wells Fargo Foundation Minnesota; and a grant from the National Endowment for the Arts. Significant support has also been provided by the Bush Foundation; Target, Marshall Field's and Mervyn's with support from the Target Foundation; the McKnight Foundation; and other generous contributions from foundations, corporations, and individuals. To these organizations and individuals we offer our heartfelt thanks.

Published by Graywolf Press
2402 University Avenue, Suite 203
Saint Paul, Minnesota 55114
All rights reserved.

www.graywolfpress.org

Published in the United States of America

ISBN 1-55597-388-4

2 4 6 8 9 7 5 3 1
First Graywolf Printing, 2003

Library of Congress Control Number: 2003101171

Cover art: Adolf Wölfli, *Giant Canary: Wingspan 10 Meters* (detail)
Courtesy Adolf Wölfli-Stiftung, Kunstmuseum, Bern, Switzerland

Cover design: Kyle G. Hunter

Contents

for BJ
and for Doc and Wilder

— But how will I find the seven-star bird?

— Open the door of the book
And sketch one on the sky you find there.

The Joke

The skeleton, my son says,
Can't cross the road because
It doesn't have the guts —

Which explains, perhaps, why
It's still at the edge of our yard
Looking out across the road, into the dark.

I'm just kidding —
You see, it's us by the roadside,
Our bones the wind whistles,
And the darkness beyond:
That's ours also.

One

Who once has lost what thou hast lost stands nowhere still.
  —*Nietzsche*

Maybe Night Comes

Sunrise over the fields
Shapes the cotton we call
Cash crop, king, snowballs in hell,
Words that hint its
Hand-shredding truth, its nighttime fellowship
With earth we eat, rain
We drink, earth we all bloom into.

Ours is the daylight world,
The dead must stay in the ground
And out of the cotton all day . . . defined,
Holdable: Cotton is King,
Its promise: to rule without
Whimsy, without contradiction . . .

But night comes like water
To obliterate and enlarge,
So that words for me — *David,*
Child, husband, lover, father —
Dissolve or spread like seeds
Over an earth where my stillborn
Brother, also David, echoes
My daily failures
With his more ultimate one.

At night, when I cannot see myself,
I see him testing an electric fence
With a blade of grass or answering
My living brother when he calls our name . . .

Maybe night comes, then,
To give us what we cannot bear to see:
Brooding over sun-cracked fields,
David, stillborn, father, name . . .

Looking for Mercy in Marion, Massachusetts

My friend who goes crazy every spring
And becomes as good as two friends
Danced in the slow water of the marsh
At sunset — such grace in his nakedness,
The cattails' waving, a new family of geese
Looping wide, wide around him.

When he came in shivering and we poured
More whiskey, he told me he'd been dancing
With my dead wife, that she'd thrown back her head,
Laughing, and burst into a flame the sun made
On the water. *Did you see her?* he said.
Yes, I said. And I leaned to him and
Kissed him year after year after year.

The Word

As brutally as bees drive their tongues to flower,
As gentle as that seems to us,
So let us live our ordinary dying,
This morning glory, this fiery star gone nod:

Here's the pure tongue of words becoming
As they also pass away: Listen, then kiss me:
The last sound we'll hear will be the silence
Of our first word finally formed, our first sweet and violent
    tasting.

God Compares the Soul to Five Things

A rose upon thorns: sweet petal bed: its toothy metallic stem . . .

A bee in honey: the sting of bee-light: the jar illumined thus . . .

A dove: in the mouth: a way of saying *I miss you* or . . . *My delicious* . . .

A sun shining . . . : *A moon full* . . . : Then:

I created you so a beginning might be made, and so too an end: this gives gravity
To the great distance between us, which is also soul. . . . Praise you.

Nights and Days

To those who are awake, there is one ordered universe common to all whereas in sleep each man turns away to one of his own.

—HERACLITUS

I

A seagull struggled a starfish skyward —
Wind wobbled and water-hung — she'd plucked it
From its salty constellation. We laughed
And our son, ever alert to failure, shouted:
Bird Brain! Starflight staggered us all . . .

Then it dropped, the tumbledown, lazy weight lost
Not to crack on the riprap seawall
But to thud, as bodies will:
The bird wandered down the air again,
Picked from the scrabble the fish and flew deep
Toward the crab hollows of the estuary's mouth.

2

As the tide pulled out and the reek revealed,
Our son wandered his galaxy of sleep . . .

Then you whispered your hand across my cheek,
And with persistence born of ignorance and want,
We dived down the darkness of mystery and feast.

The Garden

Fall's last light in the last field falls now —
A yellow butterfly. A yellow leaf . . .
Nothing we haven't lost before. In the garden

Our son speaks of the death he was born from,
That distant galaxy he knows as God — to his friend,
He whispers: *I am a messenger of God, are you?*

You laugh: *So maybe this is it — the aftermath.*
Your spade shivers as it bites the earth,
And the two boys scramble for the night's potatoes.

In the west, wandering, Venus fires its brief ascent:
A yellow butterfly. A yellow leaf . . .
Nothing we haven't found before.

The Sun Drivers

Call to the fat-bellied boy gods playing on the beach:
Try telling *them* the sun stands still!

They'll laugh at you, nestle in your arms, then whisper:
But it is we who drive it through the dark. And the moon. The
    stars.
Even this green-world wandering. The stillness lies with you
    alone.

If you could see through their eyes now,
You'd find your hair blown back, your face
Trembled by the terrible speeds of beauty born and passing . . .

Call to the boy gods, tender them a hand:
You too may take reins of bright horses and blast through the
    night.

Venus among the Wanderers

Mostly Venus wonders over what ends
And begins, unblinking lover of the in-between,
The dusk and dawn, the not-quite-being,
The nearly-night-sky, the nearly-day — she:
All is change, of course, all is
Almost — *steady, in that regard* — and,
Remembering her lovers, their
You're-not-quite-this or their
I-will-be-that-tomorrow, she says to them:
I will be yours always, this *way*, meaning
The way snow falls on water,
The way tall grass lies down for winter,
The way hard words break apart
Into the perfect, distant planets.

Death, like Faith

Death, like faith, is simple —
(Let God arise, let His enemies be scattered!)
(— Like smoke, like bars jingling
Good-night, good-night, drink up —)

All you say is, *I've had enough*, or,
Is it time already? —
Meaning nothing really, or meaning,
Nothing has worked — and then it comes to you

The way rotting fruit eases through a house,
Almost jubilant.

The Leap

To souls, it is death to become water;
to water it is death to become earth. From
earth comes water, and from water soul.

—HERACLITUS

Our son stands at the dock's edge eyeing
His other self cast on the water below:
Gulls scream, sun fires, fishes shadow
The unbearable depths, and the self-song
That calls him, calls him. . . . Then his
Explosion, the glass shatter, the bottom of the leap.

Two

Awake and sing ye that dwell in dust . . .
  —*Song of Songs*

Mr. Sweatner's Parade

Mr. Sweatner puts his cart before
His snow-eyed mule and pulls them
Down the field roads of Friendship, Texas,
Dragging cans . . .
Wake up! he cries. *Let's get on with it!*
These were the words
My grandfather used to rouse
Him and the other Mexicans who'd lived
In the wetback shed across the cattleguard.
Long ago, Mr. Sweatner's son fell from a tractor
And was baled with the maize,
And a year later his wife and child
Died in childbirth. On that night
He hammered his sixty-five chinchillas
To death and left their skinned bodies
In a pile alive with green flies.
So if he's now come back to gather
The dead Mexicans, and only them,
We ought to forgive his insolence —
Because there is no guilt here — and rather
Follow to where he takes the dead ones:
Some place still not owned, but forever theirs.

This Once Was Spring

The Friendship Memorial
String Quartet rosins
Its watery bows:
One prepares a plowshare
To bite the earth;
Another, cool soil
To soothe the wound;
A third wails wide seed on fiddle —
The last plucks an old guitar
Which echoes on the barren water.

The Founding of Friendship, Texas

The burial of Anna, age six months,
First dead in the new land,
Was a cause for celebration.
Not only had her soul — *they saw it!* —
Risen with a flock of scissortails
To join Mary's virgin train above,
But they knew, being gamblers also
On the fleshy souls of cotton and maize,
That she did not, in fact, rise
But burrowed into the black soil
To mingle with eternity here.
After a year of traveling, the family
Could finally stop, for the love of Anna
And the promise of the land
She had become, land that rose so slightly
At the San Gabriel River,
Where the only trees in sight
Shimmer a string of emeralds
On the dusty breast of Friendship, Texas.

August, the Elder

He came for the last, true
Good hope of America:

And he found it, blown dry:
The black heart of the earth
Sifting through his
Also overfarmed hands.

August! he yelled, *August!*
Demanding his birthright, his
Name's abundance, in this
The driest month.

But he only got a promise,
Like the wind's, to keep moving,
And like the wind
To move somewhere.

Sun, Moon, Stars, Rain

Ever since the dam was begun
All roads but one wind out of Friendship,
Texas, and most of those are flooded,
Bridgeless, or wrecked by mesquite or dynamite.

What's left of the jackrabbits, coyotes,
Coons, skunks, and the most stubborn ghosts
Takes a west road that is mostly clear.

My grandfather said the year the state tied ribbons
To the trees that God left on the same road,
Shaking his head, then my family, and now these . . .

The only road still leading in comes from above.
The sun rides on it, as does the moon,
The stars, and, occasionally, the rain:

These come freely to all places and never leave —
Even to the godforsaken, the soulless
And pastless, even to this shithole
Which is, at least, a place.

Birth of an Immigrant

One hundred and two years later
While pulling her last breath
From an iron tank
In the SPJST rest home, my great-grandmother,
Who smelled of the ocean
Even there, remembers milking her first cow
In Moravia and discovering both
Her power and her destiny:

When the cow kicked, grazing her forehead
And sending her reeling in the dung,
She got up, spoke kindly to the cow,
And finished filling the pail.
As she stood up from the stool
Blood from her cheek
Splashed in the milk — she picked up
A shovel, hit the cow
Between the eyes, watched
It crumple to its knees.

It was the last time she raised her hand
To anything, the last time she had to,
Since the world, the sea, and the new world
Opened up for her, a fresh furrow.

When Rozina turned to see the cow still stunned
In its broken-down shed in this her fourth home
In her seven years thanks to the Catholics
And her loudly Protestant father,
She stroked it gently and never looked back again.

Mr. Cervenka Had Time for Love

The first person to fall
In love in Friendship
Lost an arm to the first
Modern thresher,
And fresh, as always,
Made more love
Than one hand could hold.
He will forever be held
By all who needed him
In this town of hard work
Where he was the milkman,
Mailman — general utility man —
Who laughed at his nightmares
Of a town full of little,
One-armed farmers who smiled
As sweet as the devil
And might, in fact, have known him.

Aunt Mary, the Butcher: A Will

Thanks be to God and Mary
For calling to mind
The nature of all flesh:

My soul to the Almighty, yes,

But my more perfect body to the earth,
To be held in Mary's apron
While she stuffs ground venison
Into gray skins for sausage
And, in this way, provides.

Burial by Water

The river runs not so deep
That the leaves' reflections
Can't echo the wind again,
Like lovers' words the scattering
Wind, the scattering leaves . . .
All shadows of what passes,
As migrating birds —
Shrill officers of direction and next —
Flash past the river
To the fields of those who live.

Uncle Emmet, Wiser Than God

The most nearly spherical
And therefore perfect
Of seven brothers
And his beautiful, butcher-wife
Mary, brought forth
No children unto this land,
Which now is water.
They seemed to know
The dam would come
And all return to darkness,
That God would rest from then on
And say of Friendship, Texas,
I did what I could do.

Emmet laughed as they walked
Into their fields, as the water
Rose to their heads,
As Mary nuzzled his stone-smelling neck,
And he said of Friendship, Texas,
It never had a chance,
Which they'd known
Since tasting the wheat
In the body of Christ,
Since Mary first split open a rabbit
And touched her fingers to her tongue —
So they decided not to fight their destiny,
The dam's brown water of forgetting,
But rather to take it in,
To swell and dissolve like seeds,
To wander into the heart
Of that more perfect solitude:
And so, hand in hand, and slow, they did.

A Mother's Mornings

I give these mornings back to us . . .
Fog swirls over the pond, a skein of blackbirds,
A half-acre of iris blooming . . .

In our garden you stoop to gather rose hips
And teeter on your heels — a strange, dangling
Elegy your mother taught you,
As the wind blows silent
Bells of white petunias.

I give these mornings back
As if we'd shared them,
As if the sun glares on your tan, thatched hat,
The pecan tree's warblers warbling.

And I give them
In the bee-drunk syllables of regret,
Which make little sense but press us
Like the lips of our forgotten God.
Take. We can live this way.

A Confederacy

A butcher-bird sings by the flooded Nigger Flat
Along the shore of Friendship, Texas, where once,
On the iron bridge of Willis Creek, bullboys
Throttled up their trucks to celebrate
The one sad fuck worse off that night than them:
The beaten, black head lolled like a lantern.

At first just looking on, God cocked his head
Toward the faint chatter of satellites beyond,
Then, listening, stepped into the black body of man:
And the light from that body turned them, finally, all to ash:
Such were the miracles of America in those days.

These days, after the dam, the bridge is ruined,
And the cottonmouths hanging from limbs
Over the creek's steep chasm have wandered on.
We watch the sun slip down, and when the butcher-bird
Shrieks, a silence follows, a tightening in the dusk.

In the lone mesquite within the canebrake
The litter of bird's prey dangles on its thorns:
Before us the paling sky slumps onto the still, unrivered water.

The Quick and the Dead

The night the dead weren't found
Where they should have been,
The cockeyed preacher from Taylor
Stood in the back of his pickup
And shouted to the crowd: *You've had too much*
Of what you hungered for. So now He's come
To judge both the quick and the dead.

No one listened; there was a static
Over them all, and already they felt
Their bodies might rocket into the darkness above.

Almost everyone, quick and dead,
Had been moved from Friendship, Texas,
But the news that no remains were found
In the slave cemetery beside Willis Creek
Brought them back, and also the cameras,
The faithful and fearful, the sick and sad,
Even a Bechman, descendant of pioneers
Who rode their slaves like horses . . .

Under the television lights, the last to blaze
This wasteland, the geologist from Austin
Held up a diagram and explained:
Beneath the rigid crust that holds
The markers, the soft subsoil and the remains have
Migrated to Willis then on to Brushy Creek,
The San Gabriel River, Little River,
Old River, then to the Brazos which
Mingled them with Oyster Creek for miles and miles
Until they finally reached the Gulf of Mexico
Where they leapt in the air like dolphins . . .

With this the cameras snapped off,
As did the lights. The preacher, all sound,
And these new pioneers, bewildered by joy,
Followed the man through the darkness ahead.

Aeneid, Book II

The conquered have one refuge: hope for none.
All the unrebelled rally to their destiny of despair.
The beautiful bear it as a winter field bears snow.
But most of us, more clumsily heroic, bear fathers
On our shoulders, children at hand, from one
Burning city to another.

Three

O one, o none, o no one, o you:
Where did the way lead when it led nowhere?
    —*Celan*

Paint

White, he said, *I'm going to paint everything white. Good*, she said, *It's about time, it's time to paint everything white. Yes*, he said. And he pulled out a large brush and painted the words *everything* and *white* on the wall in a very attractive hand, words which happened to be the first two of the novel he'd just begun writing of the same name. She was not amused. *I'm not amused*, she said. *Paint, this place is filthy.* He painted the words *was kept in a separate room* across the wall and onto the window, then *until the snow fell and it was taken outside which is when they met . . .* and on and on until the walls were filled and the floor, the plants, the couch, the lights, the pages of books, the words, the chapters, becoming indistinguishable. She said, *The place looks great, you're a good painter. Thanks,* he said, and he took off his clothes to begin the last chapter on his legs. It was a love story, but also a mystery because it turns out the two lovers had been dead all along. *Dead people can't be characters*, she said, *It's not right.* And she took off her shirt and pants and said, *Paint, it can't end like this.* Of course, it could end any way he wanted, so he kissed her as he painted *yes* over and over until she disappeared.

Ghost

My dead wife believes in me: she's moving in the attic,
    nearing . . .
The timbers creak. I hear them! I'm here!

Good People

The woman to my left is screaming. She is screaming everything there is to scream about scream. At once she screams scream's entire and infinite vocabulary: simultaneous God- and mouse-scream, lottery-winning-, first-gray-hair-, death-in-the-family-, stars-wheeling-westward-, hard-frightening-sex-scream. And she is, in her way, handsome. She is likable. Our mothers would say she is from good people, meaning she's like us, only screaming. Our fathers would want to touch her. I do. I want to put my arm around her and say, *I understand. . . . I, too, am screaming*. She continues to scream without taking a breath. It is a lonelier-than-thou-scream. It's impressive. I find I want to raise my voice.

Father

He dies a long time and she daughters up to him: *Dead yet?* He opens one eye: *Not yet*, he says, *Still awaiting the appointed end. Who*, she says. *Exactly*, he says, *And also What.* A knot of words settles in the pine outside the window, chatters wildly about nothing. *Who will I have been*, he says. *What*, she says. *Yes, that too, but mostly Who, and then perhaps Why*, he said. *Why are those birds outside the window*, she says, *They're as noisy as books.* His thumb and finger widen his eye, *Look*, he says, *There is a great bird inside.* In the world to come she will find feathers everywhere. *Where*, she says.

Hotel

The phone rang. It rang all the time, even when it was answered, and it was answered often enough — *Hello, hello.* . . . She said, *The phone is ringing,* and he said, *I know, it rings all the time* — which is when it rang. But how it rang — through the doors, the windows, down the halls, the stairs, in every room, remained a mystery, a mystery that made them love one another all the more. She said, *I love you all the more because the phone is always ringing. Hello,* he said, *Hello.* She said, *We need an answering machine. Yes,* he said, *What could we say on it? Hello,* she said, *Hello.* Which is what he'd hoped because anything else would have disappointed and he might have even taken the phone off the hook, which wouldn't have mattered since the phone rings anyway, but which would have had symbolic significance. She said, *Do you think the ringing has any symbolic significance? Oh yes,* he said, *No question.* The message someone left on the machine was the sound of a phone ringing, which both found inexplicably exciting.

The Crying Room

In the early days, he would take her to the crying room. *You simply don't cry enough,* he said. *But I don't like to cry*, she said. *I know*, he said, *But rules are rules.* So they would walk out of town, past the waving good citizens who cried regularly, into the woods to the clear stream that leads to the crying room. Then, after walking for an hour or so, she said, *I'm awfully tired — can we rest for a minute? Yes*, he said, *We should rest before we cry.* And they would lie in the tall grass beside the stream and make love as gently as a tear sliding down his cheek. As the sun went down, the noises they made and the rising susurrus of crickets and frogs would silence the whole town's loneliness that rose from the stream like fog.

Table

He said, *I don't have anything to say to you,* and he broke his glass of milk. *I'm sorry,* she said, *What did you say?* He said, *I don't have anything to say,* and he picked up what was left of his glass and slammed it down on the table, which was now white and red. *I'm sorry, I couldn't hear you,* she said, *Did you say something? Are you deaf,* he said, and he brought down his fist on the broken glass and the white and the red. Of course, she *was* deaf, and had been for as long as he could remember, which wasn't very long because he was getting old and because she'd been dead for most of a year. *I love you,* she said. He said, *Nothing,* since he really didn't have anything to say and since he was too busy pounding the table, which, he said, would one day give way.

Revision

He looked up from the kitchen table and said, *Everyone should have killed themselves by now.* The dead woman picked up the stainless-steel-coated copper fish skillet and hit him over the head. He looked down at the table, made some notes. *Perhaps,* he said, *By now, more people might have* — she raised the pan — *considered alternatives.* It crashed on his head anyway, and blood streamed down his face like music from another apartment. He took more notes. *Your absence*, he said, *How much is there?*

The Dead

I will give you this much, he said. And he held up a giant laminated check like the ones you win at golf tournaments. *How much is that*, she said. *Much*, he said, *A great deal*. She rubbed his belly with her bare feet. *Enough*, he said, *Maybe it's enough*. *Much*, she said. He called her for days. She said, *Nothing*. He said, *I heard you were dead. Nothing*, she said, *Nothing at all. Nothing to speak of*, she said. *I'll give you this much*, he said. And he cut off an arm and a leg and gave them to her. *Thank you*, she said. And she put them under her arm as he grew smaller and smaller until he was a puddle. *I will give you this much*, he said. *Thirsty*, she said, *Thirsty*.

The Problem

Once, his body was stretched, like a tarp, over three days. She said, *I'm gonna slit open your belly.* And she did. And everything fell out: pasta, weeds, bourbon, a pocket of sparrows, pots and pans, his daughter in a tutu waving, a small bad attitude, bourbon, a sunrise swallowed one morning hungover in Greece — all of it falling for days and him stretching farther — a wad of bills, gardens, storms, broken windows, whole states, until he had stretched over a lifetime and was done: He whispered — because he couldn't catch his breath — *One must have the courage to make the last stroke that destroys everything.*

The lovers dream they've died and awakened in yellow light streaming motionless from the window: the moon an enormous clock. She says, *I've been studying how to compare this prison where I live unto the world.* He says, *I cannot do it: your body is my firmament constellating everything. I know,* she says, *My body constellates everything.*

The poem was more difficult than anyone imagined. The doctor said, *I'm afraid it had to be removed surgically, and frankly, we lost most everything: the religious implications, the soaring lyricism, the transcription of her communication with the dead, all hope. We only have the sexy parts and the ending, I'm sorry.*

Their movements were Twyla Tharpish, confused but directed, like outtakes from Capra, the edgy parts, the transitions (her hand caught briefly under his back, pulling the skin) almost improvisational, dreamlike. And he was so devoted to this confusion he couldn't distinguish the dream from the real. Through three days and nights, winter, spring, summer, tongue and moon, they loved each other, he thinks.

But his body kept spilling: engines, toys, seas, a factory's furnace lit for miles on 95 South to Florida, assorted candies, an unexplainable belief in the unbelievable, loneliness . . .

So he reaches from this world to hers, tentative, confused, laughing this dream of their bodies down his throat like a drink. It's that easy. And he drinks a lot.

Horses

All his old friends ride in on horses. They are confused because they've never ridden horses, and they are amazed at the truth of horseness — its bigness, it gracelessness in their hands. They wonder why they're there, in front of him, horsed. And they look to him for answers. He wants to tell all his old friends that they're here because he loves them, and that they're on horses because they're grown now and can ride the horses from their parents' favorite movies that they hated. But he doesn't. Instead, he climbs the wide back of his own horse and salutes them, offering them the promises they made and abandoned, the diminished fields they carry with them undiminished, and the cavalry they are that might save them.

Four

Thus swiftly passing is everything Heavenly, but not in vain . . .
 —*Hölderlin*

The Gift

Fall comes as love does: a dragonfly,
Lazy with the chill, lights on your hand —
It happens! — and, for a moment, all
That is outside comes in — just as
When we say *I love you* and are filled
With what we did not know was missing:
The orange berries of bittersweet,
The end of all endings, the tender fall
That flowers forth the world.

Aeneid, Book VI

The old ones worried less about a world to come:
To visit their dead they simply poured blood on the earth
And, gazing in the puddle, found themselves.
The message delivered, they walked into their ordinary lives.

The Crow-Trailed Fish Hawk

The crow's story,
Chattered out to crow-world,
Involves a beautiful loser
In love with both loving and losing.

Somehow, he says, *the world*
Becomes shadow, the sorry carcass
We love and feed from,
And in which, no doubt, we're too smart
To succeed much beyond surviving.

The osprey, in her silence,
Flies pride, ignorance, and mystery mixed.

Is that what you want?
Listen, my love, my shadowy otherwise:
This ash I rub on your chest laughs at the disaster of desire.

God Appears at Night as a Burning Field

All flesh is grass,
She says, naked
As the wind she stands in . . .

And its loveliness
Is like flowers
Of the field on fire . . .

Fire can't harm fire,
She says, *much less flesh,*
Which loves its flesh,

This blossom
Star, this
Machine petal . . .

Evening Prayer

For the screw, the way, straight
and crooked, is the same.

—HERACLITUS

As the driven screw winds its subtle distance
Into wood, just so your love has entered me.
As candle becomes candle when it burns, just so
This hollowing, this filling up. If my body is word,
Let it empty then. Let it fill till silent.

Elegy in Two Storms

1

She's standing at the garden's
Edge, where the land drops off
And rye grows taller before
It all lifts up to mountains at sunset.

No one understands her heart,
Or how in this storm's swaddling
Her tongue scours the low sky,
Her breath and waist — that willow — sultry and heaving.

2

She's painted white with black bone-stripes
And red circles round her eyes.
Indian, she says, *a dance for rain, in rain:*
A goldfinch flutters in her womb,
It stands on a dandelion stem, bending it over
To eat the white tufts,
Its delicate, masked head tilting back.

Thunder in August, mallow,
A pileated drumming a locust's high trunk:
Sweet mouth of earth, she says,
We eat the simplest food.

God Considers the Elements and a Bird

Fire is wood rotting — and you: I read by that light.

Water is green wood's wound hissing in the fire: my mouth.

Air is smoke, as hair becomes perfume of hair: the essence of my
love.

Earth is ash: our forgetfulness.

Rest in me as shadows rest in the body of this bird, in all things.

The Unseen, My Love

*What we saw and grasped, that we leave behind. But
what we did not see and did not grasp, that we bring.*
—HERACLITUS

All the unseen, all the forgotten:
These we carry in our haunted heads:
No room's left safely, no door's closed:

What are we kissing as we kiss . . .
This delicate remembering, this letting go . . .
Then the dazzledown your arms are . . .

The Walk

*If one does not hope, one will not
find the unhoped for, since there is
no trail leading to it and no path . . .*

—HERACLITUS

After so much talk, the weariness came —
It drove down the flowerhead, rain rent,
The star-eyes: *Nothing, not much*, you laughed,
I meant what I haven't said: such silence: we
Listened for a great distance — one word's darkness
To another to another — one bird cry flown, then another
As night yawned its great mouth over us
And forgiveness gathered as starlight in a drop of rain
And blinked — the unhoped-for joy, the secret shared:
Then these tongues, better for kissing, kissed.

Good-Bye Poem

A day comes
When you have to say good-bye,
When you point to your hand and say,

I believe this is my hand, waving.

The Star-Steered Geese of Yancy Mill, Virginia

for Donald and Doreen Davie

Hundreds of geese gathered at the cow pond
Late that late fall afternoon, their barking
Barking hard against the mountains behind them:

They were so alive the day
Seemed to dawdle in its last light
Before it gave over to the first stars
That would lead the clambering V's
Southward along the ridge.

I imagined the geese as drunken sailors
Headed for some fateful, ancient field, heroic
And loud, but now I let them go — as birds —
And think rather of those that waited behind
In the darker dark to fly in pairs, the full galaxy
Wheeling above them and the frost-lit grass below.

They were the heroes I was waiting for:
How terrifying it must have been, how beautiful.

When I think of them, I think of you,
As if your bodies, too, will pull through the air,
Be held by it, guiding by the strange fires of night.

Seven-Star Bird

And god's anger called his rivers all and told them to let
the river horses run wild as they ever would, and the
leaping rivers flooded the great plains . . .

—OVID

As breezes lap the shallow-tugged tide flow
And swallows twitter and skirt the dusk,
We lie within the wreckage of the stars —
The moon spill, our planet's pull — this sad machine.

With you sleeping against my chest,
Having drifted off as Venus began to blaze,
I feel my father's heavy breath bear
Down against my cheek, a finger toward the comet's tail:
Like a damn flashlight looking down, he said.
For three nights we watched it, then that light was out.
So we steered by the swirling mathematics
Of whiskey and revenge, the business of getting,
Then of letting go. Stars gather in the sky like rain —
Dizzy atoms that collapse, collide:

In our dream the dead of Friendship, Texas,
Stand on the shore of their once-town singing:
     Let the river horses run
     Let them run . . .

Once, in America, in full nakedness,
Our family rivered these lands with abandon —
From Moravia to Galveston to Friendship, Texas —
Their wild seeds sown, their hearts full of leaving,
They longed to stay: Abide, Abide, Reside —
But the tide comes to meet us and also to take us away:

When the dam was built to swell the rich towns south,
The flood spilled over . . .

Let the river horses run . . .

Valentinian speculation holds
That our souls, as light, are drawn to the waxing moon
Which then, upon the wane, delivers its freight
To the darker dark beyond — electrons
Finally freed into streams of gravity
Gone wild: while alone
In the dust of Palestine, sad Luria
Watches as God withdraws and so the world arises.

Let the river horses run
Let them run . . .

If, as has been said, it is our very love of God
That separates us from Him, can't we say
That the names we sketch on the churning atoms
Of this world's things, while keeping us apart,
Allow us also to love? Isn't this enough,
The shadow that we know a swallow by?

The tide flows in, the moon spill: let's
Hymn down the river, witness the wresting away:
If America drew us to a destiny of desire,
It was the outfall of a single star stunned,
Our sweet metals and machines: so
Return, exile, then return again:
Want no more than water does, low places

To dwell and the gravity to change.
And if you, too, are lost one day in loss itself,
May you trace a bird amid the mess of stars —
May you name it as you wish —
Seven-Star Bird, Lover, God —
And may its wandering guide your own.

Let the river horses run, Let them run,
Let them run wild as they ever would . . .

Notes

All of the Heraclitus epigraphs have been borrowed from the *Ancilla to the Pre-Socratic Philosophers,* translated by Kathleen Freeman.

"God Compares the Soul to Five Things": The title and the italicized words at the beginning of lines 1–4 are taken from Mechtild's *The Flowing Light of the Godhead.*

"Death, like Faith": Line 2 is from David's Psalm 68.

"The Problem": Some early lines are adapted from Giacometti's notebooks; two others from *Richard II.*

"God Appears at Night as a Burning Field": Lines 1, 4, and 5 are adapted from Isaiah 40:6–7.

"Seven-Star Bird": Isaac Luria was the creative force in the sixteenth-century Jewish mystical movement in Palestine.

The poems in this collection are related, directly or indirectly, to the flooding of Friendship, Texas, as a consequence of a dam built in the 1970s to protect richer towns south along the San Gabriel River. The town, which is now a lake, had been home to Protestant Czech farmers who had fled religious and economic persecution in Moravia late in the century before last. The names of people, living and dead, are echoed as characters here, although the stories associated with them have been altered, often utterly. This book is in honor of them, especially my grandmother, Anastasia Mikulencak Labaj, who recorded their lives and others around them before they were swept away, and whose spirit and work have guided my own.

Acknowledgments

The author would like to thank Robert Bradley, editor of Haw River Books, for publishing a number of the poems here in the chapbook *The Quick and the Dead.* He would also like to thank the editors and supporters of the following journals in which versions of these poems first appeared: "The Crying Room" and "Hotel" in *Witness*; "This Once Was Spring," "August, the Elder," "Birth of an Immigrant," and "Aunt Mary, the Butcher: A Will" in *Lilt*; "A Mother's Mornings," "God Compares the Soul to Five Things," "Table," "Nights and Days," "Venus among the Wanderers," and "Uncle Emmet, Wiser Than God" in *Agni*; "The Garden" and "The Leap" in *The Literary Review*; "The Garden" also appears at www.versedaily.org; "A Confederacy" and "Mr. Sweatner's Parade" in *Post Road*.

I'd like to thank my family for their love, support, and patience: William and Dorothy Daniel, my parents, especially, and Steven Daniel, my brother, and Neil and Jane Pappalardo, and all the Daniels, O'Brien-Pappalardos, Frosts, Lemkes, Labajs, Merricks, Mikulencaks, and Langevin-Leapleys.

I'd also like to thank my dear, dear friends—several of whom have directly helped this book take its final form, and all of whom have inspired and sustained it, though none, of course, are to blame for its shortcomings—those are all mine: Don Lee, Liam Rector, Harvey Hix, Tom Sleigh, David Rivard, Fred Marchant, Bob Bradley, Todd Lemke, Rodney Wittwer, John and Victoria Clausi, Wyn Cooper, Warren Denney, Emilia Dubicki, Mary-Beth Hughes, Joe Hurka, Marc Jacob, Paul Kingsbury, Joe and Gretchen Lovett, Tomi Lunsford, Deborah Parker, Shawna Parker, Sheila Pedigo, Daryl Sanders, Peter Shippy, Tree Swenson, the late Steve Thomas, and Abe White.

And a special thanks to Fiona McCrae, Jeff Shotts, and all the Graywolves.

My thanks also goes to the St. Botolph Club Foundation and to PEN/New England for their support.

"The Joke" is dedicated to Maximilian P. Lemke.
"Father" is dedicated to Joanne Reynolds.
"The Gift" was written for Peter Shippy and Charlotte Troyanowski.

DAVID DANIEL is the poetry editor of *Ploughshares* magazine. His poems and reviews have appeared in numerous journals, including *Agni, Harvard Review,* the *Literary Review, Post Road,* and *Witness.* He lives in Cambridge, Massachusetts, with his wife and their sons.

This book has been typeset in Stempel Garamond, a version of the original Garamond font designed by Claude Garamond, one of several great typecutters in Paris during the early sixteenth century.

Book design by Wendy Holdman
Set in type at Stanton Publication Services, Inc.
Manufactured by Bang Printing on acid-free paper.